Skateboard History of the Rinky Dink

by

John P. Boyle

Contents

Preface

This is the story of how the Rinky Dink skateboard evolved and how it was instrumental in seeding the thrill of skateboarding throughout the United States during the early 1960's. Skateboard historians concentrate their research on southern California where skateboards were first developed, but provide little information about how it became a skating sensation in the midwestern, southern and eastern United States. Many say it happened spontaneously, but are unaware of the entrepreneural efforts of individuals who first manufactured and sold skateboards in other U.S. locations. During the early 1960's, sales resistance was dominate in many states where no one had seen a skateboard or witnessed a youngster speeding along a sidewalk on a board with roller skate wheels.

It is difficult to understand how some historians report that skateboards evolved in the 1940's and 1950's when they were non-existent. Scooters were nailed together by youngsters using roller skate wheels during those decades but they were not skateboards....they were scooters with handle bars.

Historians claim Roller Derby was the very first company to manufacture skateboards in 1959, but their vice president and CFO at that time states they did not produce skateboards until 1963. During 1962, the surf shop "Val-Surf in Hollywood sold the first self produced skateboards and in that year other companies developed their first skateboards. There were no manufactured skateboards on store shelves in 1959 and it was late 1960 or 1961 before skateboards were first sold in stores. Also, many historians claim the very first skateboard advertisements were published in "Surf Guide Magazine" in 1963, but they are not aware of the Rhoades Company skateboards named Scooterbugs that were advertised in the May, June and July 1962 issues of Specially Salesman Magazine, a nationwide sales magazine with a monthly circulation of over 250,000 salesmen, distributors and sales outlets. Orders were weak at first but eventually salesmen throughout the United States began promoting and selling skateboards advertised by the Rhoades Specialty Company located in Detroit, Michigan. These first skateboards were the forerunners that belonged to the early development period of a fully developed skateboard phenomenon during 1963, 1964 and half of 1965. In July, 1965, skateboards reached a saturation point in the U.S. and sales dwindled. It appeared that most youngsters throughout the entire nation owned a skateboard and warehouses and stores were chock full of them.

More than a million Rinky Dink skateboards were manufactured in Detroit, Michigan and chain department stores like Kresge-K-marts, Macy's, Atlantic Thrift Stores, Woolworth's and many others helped create the skateboard industry throughout the United States. The events described on the following pages are the true history of how one individual and his associates helped create the nationwide sport that is part of today's culture.

Chapter One
The 1960's Entrepreneur

Johnny waits anxiously before the desk of the head buyer at the offices of a large department store corporation. Neatly attired in his very best suit, he has just finished demonstrating his new product. Too excited to eat breakfast, his stomach begins to grumble and growl. He squirms, grimaces and appears embarrassed.

The buyer, seated at his desk, holds the product at arm's length, studies it intently and begins to chuckle.

"He likes it" Johnny thinks.

The buyer places the device on his desk and his chuckle erupts into a laugh. Leaning far back in his chair, his laughter explodes into a roar and his bellows of amusement become contagious. His secretary laughs... his assistant laughs and buyers from adjoining offices peek in his office and laugh.

Johnny's suit begins to crumble and wilt just like his spirits. Suddenly the buyer stops laughing. Everyone stops laughing instantly. The buyer speaks: "No one... I mean no one in their right mind would attempt to use a contraption like this... they'd get killed! It looks like a good way to commit suicide... a real back breaker... not to mention all the rest of the bones in your body." Once again the office and hallways echo with his laughter. "No thank you!... thanks, but no thanks ! Just think of all the lawsuits ! They'd clean us out in a court of law. You'll have to do better than this if you want to sell to us. But thanks for coming in and"... he cannot finish as he throws his head back and roars once again.

Johnny retrieves his new product and places it in its cardboard box while trying to regain his composure. Between bursts of laughter, the buyer asks: "By the way, what do you call that thing?"

"Call it?" Johnny replies. "Right now I call it a skateboard,.... a Rinky Dink Surf Board! At first I called it a Scooterbug, but changed the name to Rinky Dink. Maybe I should come up with a better name.

"Better name?" laughs the buyer... "You better come up with a better... oh, never mind"... he stops, unable to continue as his body shakes with laughter.

Johnny leaves the office engulfed in the roar of laughter which is amplified in his mind by the rejection. He is devastated... He returns to his small workshop, slumps in a chair and puts his head in his hands. He can still hear the laughter.

Flashbacks of recent memories invade Johnny's mind and he reminisces about the creation of his Rinky Dink Skateboard. He thought about how he ventured from the state of Michigan to find his fortunes in the gold fields of California, but after very limited success, he wound up living in Chula Vista about eight miles south of San Diego. He found a job in the aircraft industry and worked on the afternoon shift. Every day his co-worker picked him up for the drive to the industrial factory and he always waited patiently on the sidewalk for his transportation.

One bright sunny day, while waiting for his ride he heard it far off in the distance. It was a clickety-click sound that repeated over and over. The clickety-click sounds grew louder and louder. "What could it be, he thought," as the sound approached with a rapid cadence. Suddenly, Johnny caught the glimpse of a teenager moving toward him swiftly and was astonished as the young man went flying past him, skating on a two by four board with street roller skate wheels attached to each end of the two foot long board.

"Wow!" Johnny thought. "Talk about innovation, this kid got it wired. Looks like he separated an old street skate and attached the wheel assemblies to each end of the 2 by 4 board." The grooves in the concrete sidewalk were evenly spaced about 12 feet apart and caused the clickety-click sound. "Hope he doesn't get tripped up and makes it home safely." Just then Johnny's co-worker drove up and stopped by the sidewalk so he jumped in his car quickly and before long forgot about the teenager and his clickety-click board.

The next day, Johnny waited at the very same location for his ride to work. He always arrived early so there would be no delays when his co-worker stopped to pick him up.. It was another beautiful day and Johnny was enjoying the sunshine and thinking about his home in Michigan when once again he began to hear the clickety click sound in the distance and knew the youngster on the speeding board would soon appear and fly by him again. The clicking-clicking sounds grew louder and more frequently making Johnny realize there must be more than one speeding teenager heading his way. He was right! Three energtic youths appeared not far from him, skating rapidly toward him, then zoomed on by at about 15 miles an hour. Once again, Johnny was amazed as he turned to watch them speed along the sidewalk and soon disappear in the distance.

When he turned back he saw a youngster about ten years old walking toward him, holding his board by one set of wheels and looking very sad. The skate assembly on the opposite end of the board had become loose.

"Hey, kiddo, what happened?," Johnny asked. "Looks like you need a little repair work. Let me take a look at that thing. What do you call it?"

"It's a skateboard, sir. I made it by using one of my sister's old roller skates. She's really mad at me. The nails have come loose and I can't skate on it now," he replied as he handed his board to Johnny.

"No wonder it's loose," Johnny exclaimed. "Nails won't do it. You need the roller skate wheels and metal plate attached with heavy screws or maybe small lag bolts. Hey, I saw you in my neighborhood a few days ago. I live in the house at the end of Oak street on the west corner. Stop on by tomorrow morning and I'll fix this thing so the wheels won't come off again. I have a small work shop in the garage. Here comes my ride to work. I got to go now. See you tomorrow." The youngster shouted his thanks and waved to Johnny as he jumped into his co-worker's car before they sped off.

The next morning around ten o clock, the youngster showed up with his skateboard as Johnny was working in his garage with the door open. He had a friend with him who carried a 2 X 4 board and an old-looking roller skate. Johnny greeted them with friendly words and exclaimed, "Just call me Mr. Fixit" as he inspected the young lads broken skateboard and began searching for large screws and lock washers in his tool box. After retrieving heavy duty screws and washers, he extracted the nails that held the skate wheels to the board and with a yankee screw driver attached the wheel and truck assemblies securely to the board. The youngster was elated by the sturdy construction as his friend looked anxiously at Johnny. He didn't have to ask for help as Johnny took the 2X4 board and roller skate from him and began to separate the street skate.

"I'll have you up and running in few minutes, young man," he laughed. "Your board looks a little too long. I'll saw a few inches from one end so it's about two feet long or maybe a little less. I'm quite sure these heavy duty screws will be okay, but if not, I'll use larger lag screws or nut and bolts. After you kids test your skateboards, let me know how they hold up. Come back and see me if you need any help."

It wasn't long before Johnny constructed the skateboard and handed it to the youngster, who beamed with excitement and thanked him many times. Johnny said he was only too glad to help and told the kids to have fun as they skated away after waving their appreciation once again. Johnny had constructed his very first skateboard and felt a sense of satisfaction for helping the youngsters.

As the days went by, Johnny observed many adolescents and teenagers skating along the sidewalks of Chula Vista, California. Sometimes groups of twelve or more teenagers went speeding by him as he waited on the corner for his ride to work. Suddenly a flash of inspiration hit Johnny like a bolt of lightning.

"Millions of skateboards can be sold all across the United States. I have to jump on it right now. I came to California in search for gold and here it is at my feet and it's better than all the gold I have ever found when prospecting the mountains and streams. I can sell a million or more. I got to get started immediately. It's 1960 and by this time next year I can be rich."

During the mornings on the following days, Johnny traveled to San Diego and neighboring cities to check with the managers of large department stores where he asked if any companies were already manufacturing skateboards. No one knew what he was talking about when he described all the youngsters in Chula Vista skating on home-made skateboards. They hadn't seen any in their neighborhoods, but said they would keep their eyes open for them.

After giving a week's notice, Johnny quit his job at the aircraft factory and boarded an airplane bound for Detroit, Michigan where he knew he could muster the resources he would need to begin manufacturing skateboards. He was 28 years old then and somewhat upset with himself because he had not achieved financial success after trying many entrepreneural ventures.

Chapter Two
Mr. Moore, the Machinist

Johnny's parents welcomed him home and insisted that he stay with them. Like all parents, they expressed their best wishes for his success when he explained his new skateboard manufacturing venture. Since they had never seen a skateboard or witnessed youngsters speeding along a sidewalk on a home-made board with roller skate wheels, they were a little skeptical about its success, but assured Johnny they would give him their support.

Johnny knew it would take a bundle of money to construct the metal stamping dies to form the truck assemblies needed to hold the wheels and metal plate to the boards. He realized a large rubber grommet would be needed to allow the skateboard wheels to turn when weight was applied in the direction of the turn.

After many tests, Johnny decided to use one-inch thick boards instead of two by four's and found the lighter pine wood to be more agile and just as sturdy as the heavier boards. He set up his first operation in the family's garage where he rounded the edges of the boards with a band saw, then dipped them in red paint contained in a small tank and hung on a tight line to dry. A sheet metal splash pan was installed beneath the painted boards to catch the drippings. Johnny discovered that in order to obtain a bright, smooth finish the boards needed to be dipped in a fast drying wood sealer first to prevent the red pain from fading before they were screen printed with the skateboard name.

Johnny constructed a few prototype models using new street skate parts he purchased and set out upon the task of acquiring the funds needed to begin his enterprise. He was a little surprised when the bank manager rejected his loan application for working capital and the second bank did the same, Having no serious collateral was his problem.

When searching business advertisements he noticed a small ad stating inexpensive metal stamping dies could be made by a small tool shop where the owner was semi-retired. Johnny called immediately and made an appointment to visit the owner of the die shop.

The owner, Mr. Moore, shook Johnny's hand vigorously and invited him into his office. He explained that he was 76 years old and would be able to take on small projects that did not require large heavy dies and almost impossible deadlines to meet. After examining the roller skate truck assemblies he said he could build the dies and would be able to stamp out the metal parts, but the dies alone would cost almost three thousand dollars.

Johnny gulped, then explained he only had half that amount available at the present time and asked Mr. Moore if he would accept that amount to start work on the dies until he was able to pay the balance. Mr. Moore appeared to be in deep thought for a few moments, then came up with a different plan that he offered to Johnny.

"I'm all alone here and live upstairs over my shop. I still have a few small production jobs that I stamp out for local manufacturers and it takes up a lot of my time. I intended to hire someone to assist me, but if you are interested in working off the balance owed I could apply your wages to the cost of the dies."

Johnny was elated. "Certainly, Mr. Moore. I'd be more than happy to work in your shop and apply my wages to the balance owed for the dies. I can start any time."

"Very good," Mr. Moore replied. "If you can start work tomorrow, be here at seven thirty in the morning and I'll show you how to operate the machinery. It's very simple, but maybe a little boring for a young guy like you. If you need some cash for living expenses I can apply half of your earned money to the dies and pay you the rest. Pack your lunch. The closest restaurant is over a half mile away." Johnny shook hands with Mr. Moore and assured him he would be back the next morning, ready to go to work.

Johnny arrived early the next morning and Mr. Moore showed him all the operations needed to run the production jobs. The tasks were simple and required very little training to produce the metal products. During lunch break, Mr. Moore showed Johnny many of his patented inventions that he manufactured and sold to the auto industry over the previous years. One of his lubrication devices was used on every automobile that rolled off assembly lines at a major auto manufacturer. Johnny was impressed, but rejected Mr. Moore's idea that his skateboard needed a long bar and handle at the front. It was difficult to explain that it would be a scooter then. The same type of scooter that was popular during the past few decades. Mr. Moore could not grasp the concept of skating on a board without a handle. He thought it was impossible.

Johnny worked diligently during the following month, but began to notice that little work was being done to produce his dies. Mr. Moore had taken in a few new jobs and it seemed Johnny's project had been placed on the "back burner." Age had taken its toll on Mr. Moore and many times his arthritis prevented him from working. During the next few weeks, Johnny's duties increased and soon he was doing all of Mr. Moore's grocery shopping, banking, postal and delivery activities and other tasks that were necessary to run the business. Johnny was beginning to feel like he was Mr. Moore's valet and the fact that little progress was made on his skateboard dies became upsetting. Valuable time was being wasted. Johnny knew time was of the essence and other entrepreneurs would soon be manufacturing skateboards. Johnny reasoned that Mr. Moore was dragging his feet on his dies because once they were completed, he would no longer have Johnny's support and so he purposely delayed the construction of the dies. Many times Johnny used discretion when asking Mr. Moore to complete his dies and was always given an affirmative answer, but still nothing happened.

After more than three months of faithful work and support, Johnny realized his dies would never be completed. He demanded the return of his down payment money and informed Mr. Moore he would no longer work for Mm. Mr. Moore promised he would start working on the dies immediately and have them completed within two weeks. Johnny honored his promise and remained on his job until the dies were finally completed and metal stamping machinery was in place to produce the skateboard truck assemblies.

The first production run was very disappointing. The skate trucks appeared primitive. They looked like they came from an era when making a new clothes line pole was considered state of the art, high technology. Johnny was upset. All the metal parts had rough sharp edges that would have to be ground off, then polished, buffed and chrome plated before a major department store would accept them into their line of products.

Johnny decided to skip the chrome plating after polishing the truck assemblies revealed that buffing the metal parts brightened the steel to where it would pass the quality control requirements of major department stores.

After paying for his first production run of one thousand truck assemblies, Johnny was broke. He still needed the lumber, steel wheels, axles, paint, screen printing supplies and a small industrial shop to produce his first skateboards. Once again he thought of trying to obtain venture capital, then parted company with Mr. Moore who would have to hire someone to take his place.

Chapter Three
First Skateboard Advertisements

Johnny's financial status was very low after paying for the stamping dies and the first production of the metal truck assemblies. He found a job at a die cast firm named the Tann Corporation where over 400 employees produced automobile parts for the Big Three auto manufacturers.

Johnny met the owner, Mr. David Tann, a few times when he came into the production area to solve a mechanical problem or discuss operations with the plant supervisor. Johnny admired him for his success after learning Mr. Tann started the business with only one die cast machine quite a few years ago and through his dedicated hard work expanded the business to where he was supplying Ford, Chrysler and General Motors with chrome plated die cast parts for their new automobiles that rolled off the assembly lines daily during the work week. Although Johnny received good wages, he realized it would take many months to save the money needed for his skateboard business. One again, he thought of borrowing enough money to start his venture.

Johnny's mother's surname before marriage to his father was Rhoades and she had saved money diligently from her earnings as a nurse at the local hospital. She had retired recently and Johnny was reluctant to ask her for financial aid, but one day he divulged his ambitions to her and she seemed undecided until Johnny promised to name the new company after her father who had passed away a few years earlier. His name was Phillip Rhoades so Johnny named the new company Rhoades Specialty Products Company in honor of his grandfather. Johnny's mother was elated and loaned him two thousand dollars to start his new skateboard business.

The year of 1961 was almost over when Johnny rented a small shop for $75.00 a month. It was an older building with 1400 square feet and contained a small office and a storage closet.. Two work benches had been left there by a previous renter and Johnny knew they would be very useful.

Johnny thought of advertising in national sales opportunity magazines in order to obtain salesmen and distributors in every state of the Union. He knew the lead time needed to have an advertisement published was two or three months after submitting your ad. The year 1961 was drawing to a close and if he submitted his advertisement early in 1962, it would probably be three months before his first ad would appear. The rates for display ads were expensive and at first Johnny opted for a small one-column inch ad in Specialty Salesman Magazine based in Chicago. The magazine reached over a quarter of a million salesmen and distributors. Johnny missed the deadline for the April edition of the magazine by a few days and his first skateboard ad did not appear until the May issue, which was on sale in April. His first skateboard was named a "Scooterbug" and the retail price was $2.98. The cost to salesmen and distributors was $17.98 for a dozen skateboards.

Johnny had manufactured over 300 skateboards and expected an avalanche of orders to pour in when the magazine hit the newstands and copies were mailed to subscribers. During the entire month, he received a grand total of three orders for a sample skateboard. He was devastated. He could not believe it.

"Are all the salesmen who saw my ad mentally challenged," he thought. "Don't they see the potential? Don't they realize that millions of skateboards will be sold in the future? Where is their imagination....where is their spirit of entrepreneurship?" He increased the size of the ad to two column inches for the June, 1962 edition. A good friend, skilled in art, drew a sketch of a youngster riding atop a skateboard for inclusion in the advertisement. Wow! Maybe I'll get six orders instead of three," Johnny joked. The ad cost over three hundred dollars and in 1962, it was a lot of money.

Johnny didn't realize his advertisements in a national magazine were probably the first ads to appear offering skateboards for sale. He didn't realize that his very first advertisements were instrumental in creating the multi-billion dollar skateboard business and in the near future he would manufacture and sell more than a million skateboards. The skill of skating on a board seemed to be confined to the state of California where youngsters were producing them, but throughout the mid-western, southern and eastern states, very few young people had seen a skateboard. Johnny's second advertisement in Specialty Salesman magazine began to pull in orders from sales people in almost every state in America and he was elated that finally he began to earn a profit from his creativity and hard work.

Johnny's first ads appear on the following pages. Skateboard advertisements by other manufacturers appeared months after these Scooterbug ads were first published. The ads are probably the very first advertisements that were published in a magazine with national distribution.

22 SPECIALTY SALESMAN May 1962

First advertisement for Scooterbug Skateboards.
Specialty Salesman Magazine. May 1962.

18

TYPICAL MONEY-MAKER

JUICE JUG

yours for only **50¢** if you write and ask for

Samples On Approval

Clever unbreakable plastic juice jug holds over a quart. Yours for only 50¢ if you'll ask for our tested money making salable samples as well as
COLORFUL ILLUSTRATED CATALOG
See outstanding line of cards, toys, gifts and gadgets that can make extra money for you in spare time or full time and at no risk!

PEN 'N BRUSH — Room 2-019
366 Wacouta St., St. Paul 1, Minnesota
I am enclosing 50¢. Send Juice Jug and samples on approval.
Name
Address
City_____State

19

Vintage First Skateboard
Advertisements !
(May, June, July, 1962)

Advertisements have been increased
in size for easier viewing.

Vintage Skateboard Advertisement !

(May 1962 Specialty Salesman Magazine)

Every active boy and girl, every sales outlet, a live prospect
for this new toy sensation! Kids glide fast with little effort.
You zoom at high speed---double your money with this
precision built skating marvel that's a skillful "cross"
between a skate and a scooter. Sales whiz at $2.98 retail.
Free details! Rush $2.00 for sample.

Vintage Skateboard Advertisements!

(May, June, July, 1962)

Double your money! Guide to swift success aboard the
Scooterbug, the new toy sensation that engenders
neighborhood competition so fast it will amaze you! Every
active boy and girl, every sales outlet a potential customer.
Sales whiz at $2.98 retail. Rush $2.00 for sample or get
started at once with a dozen at only $17.98. (Retail $35.76)
Free details.

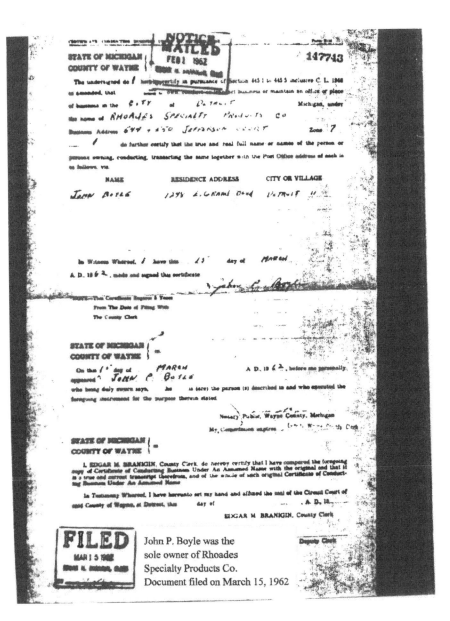

John P. Boyle was the
sole owner of Rhoades
Specialty Products Co.
Document filed on March 15, 1962

Chapter Four
The Reminiscence Ends

Johnny could still hear the laughter of rejection by the purchasing agent as he sat in his shop surrounded by his colorful skateboards. Suddenly, he stopped thinking of the past events and jumped to his feet. He walked past the 300 bright and shiny skateboards he had manufactured. Abruptly he stopped and with a look of intense determination, pounded his fist on a workbench. "I won't give up," he shouted aloud... "I'm not going to let that laughing jerk stick a pin in my bubble! Doesn't he have any vision? I'll promote it myself. I'll get it on TV. I'll try mail order. I'll pound on doors until I do sell it." He continued to pound the workbench with his fist... "I won't take no for an answer! I can do it! I know I can do it!"

During the following months, Johnny plodded along relentlessly, promoting and trying to sell his skateboards. He appeared on television teenage dance shows demonstrating his skating skills. He acquired free editorial ads in newspapers and magazines and advertised his skateboards in national opportunity magazines. He managed to sell six dozen skateboards to the prestigious J.L. Hudson Company in Detroit. The skateboards sat on the shelves. No one was buying them.

The purchasing agent at J.L. Hudsons called to ask him if he would demonstrate his skateboards at the shopping mall in north Detroit where their store was the center of attraction. Johnny agreed and they purchased additional skateboards and arranged for a story about them in the Detroit Free Press newspaper. Johnny arrived at their publishing offices at the appointed time and demonstrated his skating skills on his surfboard. He related how all the kids in California were constructing their own and the thrill of skateboarding was catching on fast. The news reporter was very impressed and wrote an excellent news article that appeared on the front page of the second section that featured local news. The Detroit Free Press had a million customers and Johnny was filled with excitement when the story appeared the next day. "A wonderful break that I needed," he thought.

Johnny was a little nervous when he arrived at the shopping mall on Saturday morning. An area had been cleared in the toy and sports departments and Johnny realized being attired in a suit and tie did not fit the occasion, so he removed his suit jacket, loosened his tie and rolled up his sleeves. When he began skating throughout the cleared section, he attracted many shoppers, especially adolescent and teenage shoppers and their parents. Cheers of applause erupted from the crowd when Johnny demonstrated his skating skills and he was no longer nervous when he spoke to the shoppers about how skateboards originated in California and were becoming very popular. Johnny's Rinky Dink surfboards began selling fast. Almost every youngster who witnessed the demonstration bought one or had their parent purchase a brightly painted red skateboard. Johnny was elated and began to enjoy his role as the innovater and manufacturer of a new skating product that was being accepted with great enthusiasm. He continued to show off his skateboards until the mall was closing. All of J.L. Hudson's stock had been sold out in one day. He knew they would be ordering more in the near future.

Johnny's advertisements in national magazines began to pull in many orders and he sold a few dozen skateboards in every state of the Union, but after all his efforts, no large volume orders were obtained and so once again he attempted selling to department stores.

One morning he entered the Kresge K-Mart buying offices, not realizing he is in their world headquarters and assumed it was their offices for local stores. He was refused an appointment. Fraught with disappointment and frustration, he leaped atop his skateboard and raced through the hallways at high speed, jumping two foyer steps and almost knocking over a large flower urn. He dodged office workers, clients, salesmen and a heavy security officer who chased him clumsily. Finally, Johnny tripped, fell and the officer pounced upon him. He grabbed Johnny by the collar and began marching him to the door. Johnny yelled "police brutality" as the burly security officer hustled him toward the exit.

The buyer of sporting goods and toys had been watching the melee with amusement and delight. He intervened, rescued Johnny from the security officer and led him to his office. Johnny thought he was in the office of the chief of security.

The buyer, Mr. Mertins asked: "What do you call that tiling? What's your name? Who is the manufacturer?"

"It's called a skateboard, sir.....a Rinky Dink skateboard" Johnny replied..."I manufacture them... My name is.... I'm sorry for the commotion I've created... I just lost it."

"Lost what? Your name?" asked Mr. Mertins as he busily wrote a purchase order for six dozen of the skateboards and handed it to Johnny.

"Here... deliver these to our test store on Outer Drive Avenue. If they sell, you'll be hearing from me. Let me have your business card. Yeah, I know... you're fresh out... another shoemaker... here, write your name and phone number on this pad." He tossed a scratch pad to Johnny. Johnny wrotes his name, address and phone number on the note pad and placed the word "manufacturer" after his name. Mr. Martins assumed it was a company name and hence the name "Boyle Manufacturing Company" was born. Johnny did not want to correct Mr. Mertins and did not mention the Rhoades name. He hoped his mother would not be upset about the name change. She was busy with her church activities and was not the least disappointed when he mentioned it.

Johnny hurried from the office building in a state of euphoria. A symphony orchestra was playing. He was walking on air a few feet above the ground. Then, for the first time he noticed the words "World Headquarters" beneath the Kresge sign. The orchestra broke into the "William Tell Overture" in his mind as he raced to his car and sped off to his shop... his old car peeled rubber. He knew the Kresge-K-Mart department stores were king of the hill with over 4000 stores. Walmart and Target stores did not exist at that time. He delivered the skateboards to the test store and helped the stock clerk place them on the shelves.

A few days later, Mr. Mertins called Johnny. "I have good news for you, Johnny. All your... what do you call them... uh...Rinky Dink skateboards have been sold. Are you set up to mass produce them in large volume?"

"Yes sir... yes, of course," Johnny exclaimed. "I can mass produce them and all I need is orders."

"Well, I'm glad of that," Mr. Mertins replied, "because I am placing you on a list to supply over 1000 of our stores throughout the United States and if you give us good service, I'll throw in another thousand stores. Okay? Can you do it?" Johnny replied with enthusiasm. "Yes, Mr. Mertins, rest assured I can do it."

Within a few days, Johnny was swamped with tens of thousands of orders from Kresge and K-Mart stores. He stared at the orders in his hand, then counted the remaining skateboards in his shop. "What do I do now?" he wondered.

Chapter Five

Mr. David Tann

Johnny knew he had to act immediately to obtain the necessary financing to fill the orders. Banks had turned down his request for a business loan earlier and he was reluctant to try again. He thought of Mr. David Tann at the Tann Corporation where he had worked previously and without hesitation he placed the Kresge-Kmart orders in hie briefcase, grabbed two skateboards, jumped in his car and headed for the Tann die cast factory.

He asked the receptionist if he would be able to talk with Mr. Tann about a business deal and she asked him to take a seat while she called to see if Mr. Tann was available for an unscheduled appointment. It was not long before the receptionist told Johnny that Mr. Tann would see him and she led Johnny to his office.

Mr. Tann welcomed Johnny with a firm handshake and asked him the nature of his business proposition. He glanced at the two brightly colored skateboards and raised his eyebrows a little before sitting at his desk. Johnny opened his brief case, grasped the orders and laid them on Mr. Tann's desk. Then he began describing his skateboards and the abundance of orders from Kresge- K-Marts and how the kids in California were making them from 2X4 boards and skate parts. Mr. Tann became very interested. He picked up the stack of orders and asked his secretary to get a total amount, then he began inspecting the skateboards. He flipped it over and took a hard look at the trucks that held the wheels to the board and shook his head. "Who made the dies that formed these wheel assemblies?" He asked. Johnny told him about Mr. Moore and the length of time that transpired before the dies were made. Mr. Tann shook his head again, but said nothing. Then he told Johnny that he could have probably bought the tracks from a roller skate manufacturer and there was no need to have stamping dies made. He asked his secretary to call the Chicago Roller Skate Corporation, then took the phone in hand. She informed him Johnny's orders totaled out at 186,000 skateboards. Mr. Tann asked to talk with the CEO and before long a friendly conversation was taking place. Before hanging up he said he would most likely call back in a few minutes with a bona fide purchasing order. Then, he called Kresge's World Headquarters and asked to speak with Mr. Mertins who assured Dave Tann the orders were valid and then they exchanged a few brief comments about a future golf event before ending their conversation. Johnny was amazed and said, "small world."

Mr. Tann explained to Johnny that the truck assemblies with wheels on a flat metal plate were available from the Chicago skate company and he was interested in funding the skateboards, but Johnny could only expect to get a royalty of 10 cents on each one sold. Johnny agreed to the business relationship and they shook hands. "I'll have my attorney draw up a contract. You can stop by tomorrow and we'll sign it."

Mr. Tann asked his secretary to bring him a Corporate Purchasing Order and to call the CEO of the Chicago Roller Skate Corporation again. He ordered a half million truck assemblies with steel wheels. Johnny almost fell out of his chair.

A woodworking company owned by George Pratt had been providing Johnny with the pine boards at two foot lengths with the ends slightly rounded for 20 cents each. Johnny gave Mr. Tann his phone number and after an agreement was reached, a semi-truck load of pine boards would be on the way to Mr. Pratts wood shop and more lumber would be delivered when needed.

Mr. Tann looked at Johnny and spoke words of encouragement. "You're going to have to take this venture and run with it. I'm too busy operating our die cast business and have little time to devote to new projects. You're going to have to wear many hats and bring everything together. You're going to have to work hard and devote all your time and energy to achieving success. At times it won't be easy and you'll have to overcome any obstacles in your path. What else do you need to get these first Kresge orders delivered?"

"Paint....wood sealer...the boards have to be dipped in fast drying wood sealer first before being dipped in the red paint, Johnny replied. "I'll need larger tanks to hold the paint. The tanks I have are too small. I'll need screen printing supplies and I might have to farm out the screen printing to another company, if I can find a reasonable price. It would expedite the manufacturing process. I'll need miscellaneous hardware like heavy duty screws, shipping cartons, yankee screw drivers.... "

Mr. Tann interrupted: "The yankee screw drivers are o.k. for starters but I'll have my engineers provide air driven devices that will speed up the operation. You'll need an air compressor installed in your shop and new paint tanks. We might have to get a larger shop later. We'll see what happens. That's all for now. I'm very busy. Good luck and keep me informed daily of your progress."

Johnny thanked Mr. Tann profusely as he shook his hand firmly before leaving his office. "I won't disappoint you, Mr. Tann. I'll get started immediately."

Johnny sat in his car for a minute before starting it. He was astonished. He could not believe the events that had just taken place. He realized that in the course of one hour Mr. Tann had spent over a hundred thousand dollars with legal bonafide purchase orders, securing the truck assemblies and lumber. He was filled with enthusiasm and excitement, knowing Mr. Tann would fund the start-up capital for his Boyle Manufacturing Company. Visions of total success raced through his mind as he drove home. "I'll work around the clock. I'll never let Mr. Tann down," he thought. "He's an amazing man....a wonderful man.....no wonder he's so successful."

Chapter Six
The Fledgling Company

It was almost midnight in an old industrial section of the city. The lights were ablaze in a small shop that was sandwiched between two old-time buildings. Johnny had been there since daylight, assembling his first production run of Rinky Dink skateboards on the workbenches. On his left, his father, brother and sister were helping and on his right multi-millionaire, David Tann, was working diligently constructing skateboards with a yankee screw driver that spun the heavy screws in place when the handle was depressed.

It wasn't about the money! It was all about the challenge! David Tann loved challenges. He always overcame obstacles. He never embraced defeat. That's why he was a multi-millionaire. He had invested over a hundred thousand dollars in the fledgling skateboard business on the spur of the moment and now he was the driving force that would guarantee the orders for almost two hundred thousand Rinky Dink skateboards would be delivered within two weeks.

There was a great divide in their social status and Johnny was surprised when Mr. Tann arrived in the early afternoon, rolled up his sleeves and went to work. Now that it was nearing the midnight hour, he was still working with vigor and Johnny was amazed at his vitality. Few words were exchanged unless it was necessary. Everyone was too busy concentrating on assembling the skateboards. On the previous day, Johnny and his brother and sister had dip-sealed, painted and screen printed over a thousand boards and now the stock of boards was getting very low.

When the clock struck midnight, Mr. Tann exclaimed, "Enough! It's time for everyone to get some rest. We'll shut it down for tonight. Tomorrow is a new day and I'll bring some additional help with me. Our production method is good for now, but it's too slow. I'll engineer a mass production method after I sleep on it. Let's lock up and go home."

Everyone thanked Mr. Tann and wished him a good night as Johnny walked with him to his auto and thanked him again. "We'll have to wood seal, paint and screen print a few thousand more boards tomorrow. Without sealing the boards first, the red paint on the boards has a gritty appearance."

"You're right, John, I'm going to sub-contract the paint and screen printing to a company that can mass produce them. It will be cheaper in the long run. Good night ! Get some sleep ! "

As Mr. Tann drove away, Johnny thought, "My gosh. I can't believe it. Mr. Tann could be on his yacht in Florida or enjoying the sunshine at the beach, but instead he's working like a teenager in this dilapidated old shop. I guess he has different values and appreciates accomplishments in the face of odds more than lounging on a beach."

On the following days, the trucks and wheels arrived by the truckload from the Chicago Roller Skate Corporation. Orders for skateboards continued to pour in. Mr. Mertins at Kresge's "threw" in additional stores like he promised. Prior to the large orders, Johnny had found the wood working company owned and operated by George Pratt, who cut the boards to size and rounded the front and back sides slightly to improve the appearance. Mr. Pratt agreed to supply the finished boards for twenty cents each and Johnny was elated because other companies quoted much higher prices. George Pratt was excited about the new business and set up a method of mass producing the boards or "decks" as they were now called. He was able to produce a few thousand boards every day and hired additional employees to more than double that amount of finished boards.

Mr. Tann sub-contracted the painting and screen printing to a large company that specialized in screen printing. The finished boards from George Pratt were delivered to the screen printing company who used electric furnaces to dry the paint quickly as the boards traveled through it on conveyor lines. Once dried, they were screen printed with the Rinky Dink Surfboard name. Everything needed to produce tens of thousands of skateboards every week was falling in place. Mr. Tann went shopping for a much larger industrial building and before long the Boyle Manufacturing Company was quartered in a hundred thousand square foot building. Every morning semi-trucks from the Kresge Corporation were waiting in line to load the previous days production for shipment to their Chicago distribution warehouse. Johnny thought, "This is a dream come true."

Each individual Kresge and K-Mart store manager ordered the Rinky Dink skateboards, but all orders were consolidated and shipped to their central warehouse in Chicago where the correct amount ordered was delivered to each store.

Mr. Tann was too busy to devote more time to the skateboard business. He called Johnny and informed him he was sending his two nephews to the skateboard shop to assist Johnny in the production and sales of the Rinky Dinks. The nephews, Allen and Jeff Tann were brothers and eager to help in all the operations necessary to produce quality skateboards.

The brothers arrived not long after Mr. Tann's phone call and after introductions, Johnny showed them all facets of the manufacturing process from start to finish. They were excited about the venture and began to help immediately. At this first meeting, the operations were still located in Johnny's small rented shop, but shortly thereafter Allen and Jeff found a much larger industrial building and Mr. Tann leased it in order to provide the room needed for mass production. Jeff and Allen had a large compressor installed to supply air power to new tools designed to fasten the trucks to the painted boards instantly. Four air-powered stations were set up in the shop and the operator at each work station could assemble three Rinky Dink skateboards in one minute. Other employees at each station placed twelve skateboards in special designed cartons and sealed them. The skateboards were loaded 'board facing board' and a sheet of pre-cut wax paper was placed between the decks to avoid scratches.

Mr. Tann's engineering department developed the fixtures needed to lock the boards in place at the assembly stations so that the automated, air driven screw driving devices could turn the screws in place with precision. The heavy duty screws were fed through plastic tubes to the magnetized bit of the screw driver. "Ingenious," Johnny

33

thought. "Mr. David Tann is a genius. This mass production assembly process is the result of his ingenuity and forward thinking."

The two brothers, Jeff and Allen, set up office procedures to expedite orders from additional large chain store retailers and orders were pouring in every day. They hired employees and Johnny trained them in the manufacturing procedures. At the peak of the metal wheel skateboard business, over forty employees worked at Boyle Manufacturing Company, located at 19750 Ralston Street in Detroit, Michigan. The company produced approximately ninety thousand Rinky Dink skateboards every month. Johnny realized he could have never accomplished this feat alone and greatly appreciated the hard work and ingenuity of the brothers, Allen and Jeffrey Tann. He realized that without Mr. David Tann and his family's support, his Rinky Dink skateboard would have never happened.

Chapter Seven
Saturation Point

During the first months of 1965, Boyle Manufacturing Company sold over ninety thousand Rinky Dink skateboards every month until the month of July. Orders were still pouring in during the month of June and it looked like there was no end in sight. However, during July, 1965, orders dwindled unexpectedly to less than five thousand skateboards. Everyone was dismayed and very disappointed.

"What happened ?" Johnny asked. Allen Tann picked up the phone and began to call customers throughout the United States. After many brief conversations, he hung up the phone and exclaimed, "It's over. The bottom has dropped out of the skateboard business. Skateboards have reached a saturation point. Every kid in the U.S. has one. Warehouses are chock full of skateboards and they're just sitting on shelves at department stores. No one is buying them. We thought it would last forever. The giant toy companies have been mass producing three times or more the number of skateboards that we have been able to make and stores throughout the entire country are swamped with new skateboards that aren't selling. Looks like it has gone the way of hula hoops. Here today and gone tomorrow!"

Johnny glanced at the stacks of cartons containing over ten thousand Rinky Dink skateboards and exclaimed, "Hope we don't have to eat them. They sure would be hard to swallow."

The saddest part for Johnny was when he had to inform all his faithful employees that the skateboard business had peaked and the shop would have to close within two weeks and all production was discontinued.. He advised everyone to begin looking for other employment. Johnny had to lay off most of the employees before the week was over.

Johnny stared at the cartons containing ten thousand skateboards and after consulting with Mr. Tann and his nephews, Allen and Jeff, he set out on a goal to sell all the remaining skateboards at a greatly reduced price of fifty cents each. Every day he traveled to stores in major cities and within a week he was able to sell every skateboard on hand to surplus stores and discount outlets. They knew sales were dwindling, but expected it to bounce back within a year. However, skateboards did not enter the sales market for almost eight years and the metal wheels were no longer used since the larger polyurethane wheels provided much better traction and greater control. The boards or decks were much wider and a new brand of skateboards evolved.

Within two weeks, the Rinky Dink skateboard shop was closed and all sales were discontinued. Johnny thanked Mr. Tann and brothers, Allen and Jeff for their financial support and hard work before parting company. "It's o.k." he thought. "Another 'skateboard' venture will come along in the future."

Afterthoughts

It may be difficult for younger readers to understand how a profit could be made from the sale of the Rinky Dink skateboards when the retail cost was $2.98. It would seem the cost of wood boards, paint, wood sealer, screen printing, truck assemblies, fasteners and labor would have prohibited any profit whatsoever.

However, during the early 1960's an entirely different economy was firmly in place. The average cost of a new car was around $2,700 and gasoline ranged between .27 cents and .31 cents a gallon. The minimum wage was $1.25 and annual salaries in manufacturing was around $5,500. A Hershey bar cost a nickel and you could send a letter by first class mail for .4 cents. A ticket to your favorite movie ranged between 25 cents and one dollar.

The following list of commodity prices demonstrates the difference in costs compared to the price of the same items in today's economy.

Six pack of Pepsi......59 cents.	New Home.....$ 12,700
Fast food burger........20 cents.	New Auto Tire.....$ 15.00
One dozen eggs........32 cents.	Monthly rentals....$115.00
Frozen TV dinner.....39 cents.	8 ft. 2x4 board.....$0.55
Loaf of bread...........21 cents.	8 ft. 1x4 board.....$0.42
Sugar. Five pounds.....38 cents.	Paint, one gallon $3.75
Motor Oil quart.....25 cents.	Skate trucks.....$0.24 each

The prices in this list may vary a few cents in different localities, but they represent how Rinky Dink skateboards could be produced and sold at the retail price of $2.98.

John P. Boyle was perhaps the very first individual to design, manufacture and sell skateboards. During 1960 and 1961, while living near San Diego in Chula Vista, California, he helped neighborhood youngsters attach skate wheels to various size wooden boards and skate on sidewalks and downhill slopes. He became a proficient skater and recognized the sales potential of skateboards.

He returned to his home in Michigan where he obtained funding from his mother, Ruth E. Rhoades, to begin manufacturing skateboards and named his company Rhoades Specialty Products Company in her honor. He had stamping dies built to form the truck assemblies and used metal street skate wheels.

His first skateboards were named "Scooterbugs" and advertised in the national sales magazine, Specialty Salesman, in their May, June and July issues. Sales from these ads were weak and his attempts to sell skateboards to national chain department stores were met with resistance. One store buyer laughed boisterously and stated, "No one in their right mind would attempt to skate on a contraption like this." Other buyers joked that "It looks like a good way to commit suicide" or "this thing is a real back breaker...no thanks."

During 1962 and 1963, John promoted his skateboards by demonstrating them at the Northland Shopping Mall in Michigan, obtained newspaper editorials and skated on teenage TV dance shows. He succeeded in selling small quantities to local stores and the J.L. Hudson Company.

When skateboarding became popular in 1964 and early 1965, John developed the "Rinky Dink" skateboard, started Boyle Manufacturing Company and sold over one million skateboards to national department stores like Kresge-K-Marts, Woolworths, Macy's, Hudsons, Atlantic Thrift Stores, etc., etc.

These very first skateboard advertisements are unique memorabilia in the history of skateboarding.

The Rinky Dink Skateboard!

During early 1961, John P. Boyle returned to Michigan after helping youngsters in Chula Vista, California construct home-made skateboards from roller skates and boards.

He began manufacturing the Scooterbug skateboard at Rhoades Specialty Products Company and advertised them in the May, June and July, 1962 issues of Specialty Salesman Magazine. In late 1962, he founded Boyle Manufacturing Company and changed the name of his first skateboards to **Rinky Dink Surf Boards** and promoted them throughout the mid-west and eastern United States.

Boyle Manufacturing Company was located at 19750 Ralston Street in Detroit, Michigan where over one million Rinky Dink skateboards were manufactured and sold. The company employed over 40 people at the peak of skateboard sales in 1964 and 1965.

Many other companies produced the original skateboards of the 1960's and in July, 1965, it reached a nationwide saturation point and sales were diminished, resulting in the close of many companies, including Boyle Manufacturing Company.

Made in the USA
Middletown, DE
18 December 2019